"Cathy Taylor has a heart for people I have rarely seen before. She is very involved in a large national ministry, yet has always made time for the hurting person, no matter how long it takes. She is fantastic at balancing the practical with the ideal. I have heard many testimonies from those who have been personally touched by Cathy, many who believe she was the turning point in their lives. This curriculum shows her incredible heart...and also her unsurpassed ability to share concrete, understandable steps and tools to bring you to where you need to be. Much of church emphasis seems geared to motivate us to seek an ideal, but after the initial enthusiasm wears off, we wonder what comes next. Not so with Cathy. She gives both the vision and the road map for the long journey ahead.

I am overjoyed to call her my friend."

Bret Lewis
Former Los Angeles NBC and CBS TV sportscaster.
Leader of Celebrate Recovery ministry at
Bel Air Presbyterian Church

"It has been a life changing journey knowing Cathy Taylor and I wholeheartedly recommend this amazing woman of God and what she has to offer in **Hurting Moms, Mending Hearts**. I have seen her commitment and passion and her willingness to be used by God in everything she does. Given the opportunity, Cathy Taylor and the work she has done with **Hurting Moms, Mending Hearts** will change lives."

Jo'El Ramirez
President of JHR Management Company
Host of Joy In My House inspirational reality radio show

"My name is Dusty Marshall and I am the President of the nonprofit Christian ministry Irregular4Christ. Cathy Taylor is one of our biggest supporters from the standpoint that she understands recovery, and wants to come alongside those who are trying to better the lives of others who are struggling with hurts, habits, and hang-ups. Her heart for the lost and broken is second to none.

Over the past two years, she has helped open so many doors for our ministry to reach other struggling addicts. Her work is hands on as she devotes her time and attention to making sure others needs are taken care of. She is a friend and an amazing woman of faith. With that same spirit, she has developed **Hurting Moms, Mending Hearts** which I would highly recommend to anyone with wayward children!"

Dusty Marshall
Irregular4Christ

Hurting Moms
mending hearts
Breaking Free

Copyright © 2015 by Cathy Taylor

SQUARE TREE PUBLISHING
www.SquareTreePublishing.com

---▶ For More Information

SQUARE TREE PUBLISHING
info@SquareTreePublishing.com
www.SquareTreePublishing.com

To contact the author or for bulk book orders:
www.SquareTreePublishing.com

---▶ Scripture References

---▶ Cover and Interior Design

Cathy Nelson Arkle - The Thumbprint Group

ISBN: 978-0-9903190-2-3

Welcome Letter From Cathy

You have recognized your need for help because your child is making poor choices, has become estranged from your family, or is living in a way that could ultimately lead to his or her destruction. You are a **Hurting Mom**.

As a **Hurting Mom** myself, I have experienced the heartache and pain of watching my child completely rebel against me and our family and I understand the overwhelming pain, and the guilt and shame that you feel as you try to figure out what went wrong.

My prayer for you as you participate in this group is that you will be encouraged and given hope and that you will learn to accept and embrace the perfect peace that God wants for you. As you talk about your situation in a safe place with other **Hurting Moms** you will begin to heal as you surrender your child to God. He loves your child infinitely more than you do. You will come to understand that you are not alone as you listen to other stories that sound a lot like yours. There is something special that happens when moms who are going through the same hurt and pain share with one another, listen to each other and pray for each other and the children that brought them together.

As you gain healing, hope, and understanding, my desire is that you will pass on what you learn to other moms who are suffering with the same pain you have experienced so they, too, may find freedom. In fact, the goal of this program is found in 2 Corinthians 1:3-4 which says, *"Praise be to the God and Father of our Lord Jesus Christ, the Father of compassion and the God of all comfort, who comforts us in all our troubles, so that we can comfort those in any trouble with the comfort we ourselves have received from God."*

My prayer for you is that you will experience not only healing as you work your way through this curriculum, but that you will also develop a closer, more intimate relationship with Jesus Christ.

Cathy, her husband Jeff, and their blended family

Dedication

I dedicate this work to my daughter, Leah.

God has brought us full circle and today

I couldn't be more proud of you or more

grateful for the loving relationship

we share.

Acknowledgements

I would like to thank and acknowledge the following people for making this curriculum possible:

▸ My sister, **Beth Aboites,** for planting the seed and encouraging me to publish this work.

▸ My Brother-in-law, **Robert Aboites,** for creating the branding (logo) and for his support and instruction.

▸ **Pastor Gene Pietrini** for finding some awesome leaders and pioneering the **Hurting Moms** curriculum at Cottonwood Church.

▸ **Sherry Ward** for her vision, for believing so enthusiastically in this curriculum and for the generous investment of her resources, time, and creativity.

▸ **Rhonda Love** for her amazing leadership in multiple **Hurting Moms** groups and for her support, in sight, encouragement, and love throughout this process.

▸ **Felicitas Ramierz** for the first Spanish translation of the **Hurting Moms** curriculum, for leading multiple groups in Spanish, and for her support, encouragement and insight.

▸ **Ron Roberson** for his generosity in sharing his expertise by filming and editing hours of footage of **Hurting Moms**.

▸ **Scott Moore** for taking time out of his busy day to take photos in the park.

▸ **Cathy Arkle** for sharing her incredible talent by creating the artwork for both inside and outside of the book. She was spot on with the ideas she presented and I am so grateful for the way she captured the essence of the program.

▸ **Melodie Fox** for editing the content and making sense of my words.

▸ **Jackie Priestley** for the final editing of the work books and the Leader Guide.

▸ **Travis Williams** for formatting the sessions in a way that made them both attractive and inviting.

Purpose Of Hurting Moms, Mending Hearts

▸ Each **Hurting Moms, Mending Hearts** (HMMH) support group provides an opportunity for hurting moms to come alongside of one another as they bear the pain, learn to understand the struggle that they are going through, and offer insights learned from their own experiences to those who need it.

▸ Each HMMH group hopes to challenge members to grow in their relationship with Jesus as we learn to trust Him in the midst of our pain.

▸ The ultimate goal is for each individual **Hurting Mom** to learn to surrender their children to God, knowing that He created them, loves them and has a plan for their lives.

About Cathy Taylor

Although Cathy Taylor grew up as a pastor's daughter, she didn't accept Jesus as her personal Lord and Savior until the age of fifteen. At eighteen she married her first husband and spent the next 30 years in and out of relationships, living her life far from God. After being divorced three times, she met her current husband, Jeff. Life with Jeff was filled with chaos and turmoil for the first six years due to the alcohol that they both consumed on a daily basis. But it was Cathy's children who suffered the most. When Cathy and Jeff stopped drinking and recommitted their lives to Jesus in 1998, the damage had already been done. One of her daughters was totally out of control.

Cathy's pain and desperation, and recognizing that she had no control over her daughter's choices, drove her to earnestly seek God's peace and comfort. As she grew closer to God and began to see herself the way He sees her, she was able to accept His forgiveness for what her life had been and for her part in what was happening in her family. She was able to forgive herself, move beyond her guilt and shame, and completely surrender her daughter to Jesus.

As she experienced healing in her own life, Cathy began to think about other moms that might be going through similar circumstances. She wanted to share with them what God was teaching her about letting go and accepting the peace and comfort that only He can provide. Out of her desire to help other hurting moms, the idea of a **Hurting Moms, Mending Hearts** group was born. She started a support group at her church in Long Beach, California, where simply by sharing and listening, hurting moms could find healing. The success of that first group convinced Cathy that there was a definite need for this kind of support which inspired her to write this material.

Cathy's hope is that **Hurting Moms** all over the world would find relief by trusting God with the pain and concern they have for their children and through sharing, mending hearts would be the lasting outcome.

Table Of Contents

Support Group Elements

Opening Prayer

Each weekly meeting will start with prayer. This helps us to clear our minds and to set aside the business of our day as well as to open our hearts to what God wants us to hear and learn during our time together.

Key Scripture

Every week Scripture will be used throughout the lesson as the basis or foundation of what we are learning. We will start each session with a key verse that is relevant to the week's topic of conversation.

Sharing

Hurting Moms, Mending Hearts provides a safe place to talk about something that is extremely painful and, for some of us, also very shameful. We know that everyone in the room is going through feelings and emotions similar to ours and that gives us the courage to open up with one another as we share our deepest hurts. By talking about our pain, we begin to experience freedom from the power it has had over us. It is a wonderful thing to realize that we are not the only mom who is going through the agony of having a child who is out of control. As we listen to other hurting moms tell their stories we begin to find strength in the fact that we are not alone. Lifelong bonds and friendships are formed in this group and you are encouraged to share your contact information and to reach out to one another during the week.

Video

Many hurting moms have received healing and hope by participating in a **Hurting Moms, Mending Hearts** group. Some of them have recorded their experience in order to encourage you along this journey. Each week you will watch a short video segment of a hurting mom telling part of her story. As you hear their stories you will come to understand that you are not alone and that there is hope for you to once again experience peace and joy in your life.

Discussion

Each week we will be learning about different elements of being a hurting mom. We are all experiencing various levels of pain and we may have a hard time identifying exactly what we are feeling or how the situation is affecting us. As we work our way through this workbook we will begin to understand how to deal with our emotions and how we can love our child, without allowing them be in control of our lives or the lives of our other family members. Ultimately, we will learn how to break free of the pain by surrendering our child to God and opening ourselves up to receiving the peace that he wants to give to us.

Support Group Elements

Activity

We will take what we learn each week and apply it to our lives in some practical way and then share that with the group. These activities will deepen the experience and help to set you free from the negative emotions associated with having a child that is making poor choices and doing self-destructive things.

Moving Forward

Each week you will be given an activity to work on during the week in order to deepen your experience with the ideas that were shared. Although the activity is optional, it is highly recommended and designed to help you get to the next level of healing and hope. Each week you will also find quotes in your workbook from other hurting moms that will give you encouragement as you move forward.

Closing Prayer

We will end each week by praying for requests and concerns that the individuals in the group may have. Group members are also encouraged to pray for each other throughout the week.

Preview of Next Week

At the end of each session you will be given a quick overview of the discussion topic for the next week.

Group Guidelines

▸ Whatever is said or prayed about within the safety of our group will remain confidential with its members.

▸ When someone else is speaking, listen without interrupting. This includes trying to comfort someone who is crying. There is healing in tears and we want to allow them to flow.

▸ We are here to encourage, support, comfort, and uplift one another. We are not here to judge one another or fix each other.

▸ Although there will be times when it is necessary to be flexible, we will keep our sharing to a five (5) minute time limit in order to allow everyone an opportunity to share.

▸ You are encouraged to bring your Bible to the group as we will be going through Scriptures each week. The group leaders will have extras Bibles on hand in case you do not have one.

▸ Group members are encouraged to continue their relationships with one another outside of the group.

Resources

Website

www.HurtingMoms.com

Email

info@HurtingMoms.com

FREE Daily encouraging words for Hurting Moms.

Cathy Taylor has put together words of encouragement using some of the Scriptures that have inspired her along her journey as a Hurting Mom. She hopes that they will bring you comfort and peace as you go through your day.

Sign up at *www.HurtingMoms.com*

⋯▶ Recommended Reading

▸ **A Journey Out of the Wilderness** by Sherry Lynn Ward

▸ **Closing the Door, but not my Heart** by Trenda Lineback

▸ **Daring Greatly** by Brené Brown

▸ **Praying for Your Adult Children** by Stormie Omartian

⋯▶ Recommended Websites

▸ www.BlueLetterBible.org – For Bible verses and original language

▸ www.SquareTreePublishing.com

SESSION ONE
Getting Started

----> Opening Prayer

----> Key Scripture

"Praise be to the God and Father of our Lord Jesus Christ, the Father of compassion and the God of all comfort, who comforts us in all our troubles, so that we can comfort those in any trouble with the comfort we ourselves receive from God." – 2 Corinthians 1:3-4

----> Video

"Hurting Moms, Mending Hearts
helped me by allowing me to surround myself with other moms going through the same thing I'm going through. It gave me a sense of empowerment. It gave me sisterhood! It gave me a place where I can be transparent!"
– Regina

Scan to see Video

----> Discussion

Getting Started

⟶ Sharing

What brought you to the **Hurting Moms, Mending Hearts** group? Please feel free to share whatever you feel comfortable discussing. Remember, your story is important.

As you watched the video, what stood out to you? How were you encouraged by what you heard?

⟶ Encouraging Verses

Scriptures that will comfort and encourage you have been provided. The Word of God gives us hope even when we feel helpless and hopeless in our situation. I encourage you to read these and other passages throughout the week. We have HMMH Scripture Cards available in the Hurting Moms store at www.HurtingMoms.com.

⟶ Activity

Let each of us take turns reading the Scriptures aloud. As we go around the room, share which verse seemed to mean the most to you.

Getting Started

⟶ Moving Forward

These are some of the ways you can move forward this week. You can do as many of these as you would like. They are meant as suggestions to help you move forward in your healing process.

- ▸ Read the scriptures on the following page aloud this week.
- ▸ Memorize at least one of the verses.
- ▸ Journal - Journaling is a great way to express how you are feeling on paper and can be a very freeing exercise. You can journal every day or only on days that you feel like doing it.

"The Scriptures are important because they lift you up when you're down and make you remember that God is always with you." – Xochitl

⟶ Closing Prayer

Exchange contact information, along with the names of your children, with the other members of your group so you can begin praying for them. A sheet is provided at the back of your book. We highly recommend encouraging each other throughout the week.

⟶ Preview of Next Week

PHASES OF PAIN AND GRIEF – PART I – Next week we will be discussing the phases that we go through as parents when we realize that the children we love have turned toward self-destructive behaviors.

"Praise be to the God and Father of our Lord Jesus Christ, the Father of compassion and the God of all comfort, who comforts us in all our troubles, so that we can comfort those in any trouble with the comfort we ourselves receive from God." 2 Corinthians 1:3-4

The Lord, *"heals the brokenhearted and binds up their wounds."* – Psalm 147:3b

"The God of all grace, who called you to His eternal glory in Christ, after you have suffered a little while, will Himself restore you and make you strong, firm and steadfast." – 1 Peter 5:10

"Cast all your anxiety on Him because He cares for you." – 1 Peter 5:7

"Do not fear, for I am with you; do not be dismayed, for I am your God. I will strengthen you and help you; I will uphold you with My righteous right hand," says the Lord. – Isaiah 41:10

Jesus said, *"Peace I leave with you; My peace I give you. I do not give to you as the world gives. Do not let your hearts be troubled and do not be afraid."* – John 14:27

"Be strong and courageous. Do not be terrified; do not be discouraged, for the Lord your God will be with you wherever you go," says the Lord. – Joshua 1:9b

Pick a Scripture that spoke to your heart.

_____

_____

_____

_____

_____

_____

_____

_____

_____

_____

What did this verse mean to you?

_____

_____

_____

_____

_____

_____

_____

_____

_____

_____

_____

_____

_____

_____

Prayer Requests

Name: _____

Situation: _____

_____

_____

_____

_____

_____

Name: _____

Situation: _____

_____

_____

_____

_____

_____

Name: _____

Situation: _____

_____

_____

_____

_____

_____

Name: _____

Situation: _____

_____

_____

_____

_____

_____

SESSION TWO
Phases of Pain and Grief - Part 1

----> Opening Prayer

----> Key Scripture

"*We wait in hope for the LORD: He is our help and our shield.*"
– Psalm 33:20

----> Sharing

Share one of the Scriptures that really stood out to you last week.

----> Video

"***Hurting Moms, Mending Hearts***
*helped me to forget about what I'm going
through...being able to share the pain
together with other HM. We cry together
and pray together and it gives me hope!*"
– Felicitas

Scan to see Video

----> Discussion

9

Discovering Our Current Phase of Pain and Grief

We are all here because we are moms and we are in pain. The pain we are experiencing is caused by many factors related to the children whom we love:

▸ Our kids are hurting and seem to be destroying themselves.

▸ Our kids are rebelling against us.

▸ Our kids are manipulating us.

▸ Our kids don't understand or appreciate all we have done for them.

▸ We feel as though we have failed as parents.

▸ The "if onlys" creep into our thoughts on a regular basis.

▸ It seems as though everyone else's kids are perfect and we feel ashamed and embarrassed.

▸ We are tired of trying to fix, repair and restore our kids all the things that they are messing up.

▸ We feel helpless with regard to what to do make things better for our kids and ourselves.

⇢ **Circle the ones above that apply to you. Share with the group.**

As we begin to realize that our child is out of control our dreams for them and for our family become broken or fragmented. We begin to experience tremendous loss and we can't move on in our own lives until we go through a process of grieving for what was or what might have been. This process has several phases but it is important to interpret these phases loosely. There is not an orderly progression from one phase to the next and it is common for us to experience the phases out of order, have them repeat themselves, or even to have multiple phases hit at the same time.

The important thing to remember is that it is perfectly normal to grieve for the sense of loss we are experiencing regarding our child and we need to allow ourselves the space to do so.

Let's take a look at the phases of grief.

Phases of Pain and Grief

Shock Phase:

- ▶ Our child has brought us into a world of pain.
- ▶ It may have crossed our minds that something was wrong, or it may have come as a complete shock.
- ▶ We vary in the strength of our reactions, but we all feel stunned and distressed.
- ▶ The Shock Phase is usually fairly short and can last for hours or days.
- ▶ The more dramatic or severe the situation, the greater the shock and the more we become paralyzed and numb.

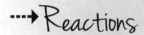 ## Reactions

Retaliate, Battle, or Run
- ▶ This is called the "fight or flight" instinct.
- ▶ The better, and by far the healthiest, way to deal with the situation is to face it and work to regain control.
- ▶ Running from the difficulty of the situation does not help and it will most likely extend the crisis.

Dazed and Confused.
- ▶ Our thinking is disoriented.
- ▶ We are often unable to make decisions.
- ▶ We feel overwhelmed and unable to move.

Look for what seems to have vanished
- ▶ A lot of times during this phase we begin to look back and remember how our child use to be or what once was.

Actions

The best and most healthy thing we can do is to talk about how we are feeling as often and as much as possible.

- ▶ Talking about our hurt and sharing the details about what has happened helps to take the power out of it.
- ▶ Another way to cope with our pain is to get busy physically. We can work out, clean the house, run, cook, whatever has brought us pleasure in the past.

It is important that in this phase that we spend time with nonjudgmental and accepting people who will listen to us.

- ▶ People who are compassionate and sympathetic make the best listeners and will help us the most.

Most of us have come through this shock phase. What are some ways you handled the shock phase?

Bewilderment Phase:

▸ During the Bewilderment Phase we feel emotionally drained.
▸ This phase will probably last longer than the previous phase – it could last for days, weeks, and in some cases, months.
▸ During this phase we tend to deny what we are feeling and our feelings are often unpleasant, even ugly.
▸ Our emotions seem to feed off of one another.
▸ We can expect that these phases will often overlap with each other.

 **Reactions**

Our reaction during this phase is emotional.
▸ We probably feel angry, frightened, and ashamed.

Our thoughts are unclear and unreliable.
▸ We don't know what to do.

We go back and forth between making deals in our heads and distancing ourselves.
▸ Making a deal can take the form of thinking about how it "could have been" and "if only".
▸ We try to pull away physically and emotionally from our child.
▸ We try to defend ourselves against the hollowness that this adversity brings.

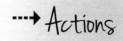 **Actions**

We need direction and support from others.
▸ It is important that we allow compassionate friends and family to help us get our lives back on track.
▸ We must be cautious not to be too tough on ourselves at this time.

Discovering Our Current Phase of Pain and Grief

→Activity

Circle the statement(s) from Session 2 that are most relevant for you today.
Share one of them with the group.

→Moving Forward

Spend some time thinking about the phases we discussed.

▸ Which phase best describes where you are right now?

▸ What positive steps have you taken or can you take as you move through this phase?

*"Going through this phase, I never thought my family would go through this.
It took me by surprise. I didn't know what to feel or think."*
 - Felicitas

→Closing Prayer

→Preview of Next Week

PHASES OF PAIN AND GRIEF – PART II – Next week we will talk about two more phases of pain
and grief and where we are in this process.

Moving Forward Journal

Which phase best describes where you are right now?

_____

_____

_____

_____

_____

_____

_____

_____

_____

_____

What positive steps can you take as you move through this phase?

_____

_____

_____

_____

_____

_____

_____

_____

_____

_____

_____

_____

_____

Prayer Requests

Name: _____

Situation: _____

_____

_____

_____

_____

_____

Name: _____

Situation: _____

_____

_____

_____

_____

_____

Name: _____

Situation: _____

_____

_____

_____

_____

_____

Name: _____

Situation: _____

_____

_____

_____

_____

_____

SESSION THREE
Phases of Pain and Grief - Part II

····→ Opening Prayer

····→ Key Scripture

"See, I am doing a new thing! Now it springs up; do you not perceive it?" – Isaiah 43:19a

····→ Sharing

Which of the phases that we discussed last week best describes where you are today? What other phases have you experienced in your journey as a **Hurting Mom**?

····→ Video

"In the shifting phase, I realized I did not have control. I totally put the control in Gods hands and released it to Him."
– Adrienne

Scan to see Video

····→ Discussion

Shifting Phase:

▸ We are shifting our focus to our other children, our spouses and our job.

▸ We will most likely be in this phase for quite a while - weeks or evens months.

▸ It is vital that any important decisions we make wait until we begin to experience hope and confidence.

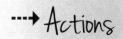 ## Actions

We begin to feel optimistic.

▸ Although some degree of depression may come and go, we begin to look ahead and talk about the future.

▸ Our emotions and our responses are hopeful

We can participate in figuring things out.

▸ We have a new awareness that allows us to take counsel from others and make plans.

We are looking for fresh experiences in our life.

▸ New connections can include a small group, serving others, or a richer relationship with Jesus.

Spiritual Direction is what we need the most at this time.

▸ Begin to look for guidance and answers by reading the Bible and praying.

Re-Building Phase:

▸ This will be the lengthiest phase.
▸ We can now decide not to feel sorry for ourselves any longer.

----▸ Actions

We experience the re-appearance of anticipation and courage.

▸ We are once again confident, able to think ahead and to make plans.
▸ We begin to have interest outside of our home and family.
▸ We start taking care of ourselves (exercise, new hairdo, etc)

We feel excited about life, which is a signal that the pain is coming to an end.

▸ We are ready to connect with friends
▸ We look for ways to serve others.

----▸ Activity

▸ Have you entered any of these phases yet?
▸ What are some specific actions you can take as you begin to shift and re-build?

····▸ **Share with the group.**

⟶ Moving Forward

▸ Use some of the tools you've gained to write an encouraging note to yourself.
▸ Be prepared to share it with the group next week.

> *"When I did this activity and wrote an encouraging note to myself, I felt very secure, safe, and hidden in the love of the Father."* – Rhonda

⟶ Closing Prayer

⟶ Preview of Next Week

EMOTIONS WE ENCOUNTER – Next week we will talk about the different emotions we experience as a **Hurting Mom**. We will explore together what the Bible says about those emotions.

Write an encouraging note to yourself.

Prayer Requests

Name: _____

Situation:_____

_____

_____

_____

_____

_____

Name: _____

Situation:_____

_____

_____

_____

_____

_____

Name: _____

Situation:_____

_____

_____

_____

_____

_____

Name: _____

Situation:_____

_____

_____

_____

_____

_____

SESSION FOUR
Emotions We Encounter

---▸ Opening Prayer

---▸ Key Scripture

"All Scripture is God-breathed and is useful for teaching, rebuking, correcting and training in righteousness so that the servant of God may be thoroughly equipped for every good work."
– 2 Timothy 3:16, 17

---▸ Sharing

Share the encouraging notes you wrote this week.

---▸ Video

"My biggest fear was that my kid would die. Three of them were all addicted and it was difficult to manage. I didn't want to lose any of them!" – Leticia

Scan to see Video

---▸ Discussion

We cannot control the actions of our child. However, we can control our reactions to them. Some of us react by trying to mask our pain with alcohol or drugs. FFor others, our way of reacting and coping with the hurt we are experiencing is through shopping, eating, working, sleeping, or jumping from relationship to relationship. Some may sink into depression and want to sleep away the pain. Regardless of what we do to medicate ourselves, Scripture shows us that our reactions to our child's behavior can cause us to feel separated from God. Our feelings contribute to how we are reacting. We are instructed time and time again to put our trust in Him and to control these damaging reactions.

We need to let God come close to bear our burdens and share in our pain. His presence will be reassuring and strengthening. Psalm 68:19 says, *"Praise be to the Lord, to God our Savior, who daily bears our burdens."* Matthew 11:28 Jesus said, *"Come to me, all you who are weary and burdened, and I will give you rest."* These Scriptures are the answer to our heartache, but we need to let go of the baggage of our negative reactions. This may be easier said than done, but again, Scripture says, *"I can do all this through Him who gives me strength."* – Philippians 4:13

Disappointment

Disappointment produces negative feelings and attitudes. For some of us it can lead to depression. Disappointment digs deeply into a person's sense of well-being. The Bible says that if our hope is in the Lord we will not be disappointed.

- ▶ Romans 5:5
- ▶ Psalm 73:26
- ▶ Isaiah 49:23b

Anger

Anger and resentment often exist in close proximity. While anger may at first be a natural and healthy response, if it is not dealt with and resolved, it can burrow into a person's life and take up permanent residence. God's instructions regarding anger are made clear in the Bible.

- ▶ Psalms 37:8
- ▶ Proverbs 29:11
- ▶ Ephesians 4:26
- ▶ Colossians 3:8
- ▶ James 1:19-20

Hurt

Even though we have not been hurt physically, we can be left reeling emotionally when hit where we are most vulnerable. Although we are experiencing incredible pain it is important to remember that we have a God who loves us so much that He hurts with us. We can be somewhat comforted knowing that we are not alone and that one thing we can do is talk to God about our situation and our children.

- ▶ Psalm 147:3
- ▶ Psalm 69:29
- ▶ Psalm 119:50
- ▶ Luke 6:28

Emotions We Encounter

Discouraged

We become discouraged when we find ourselves helpless to change a situation. We used to be able to direct where our child went, for how long, and what time they should come home. Now we find that we have no control; we are powerless over the behavior of our children.

- ▶ Deuteronomy 31:8
- ▶ Joshua 1:9
- ▶ Psalm 42:5

Fear

We are often afraid for the safety of our child. We worry about what will happen to them if they continue on this destructive path.

- ▶ Psalm 27:1
- ▶ Psalm 34:4
- ▶ Psalm 56:3
- ▶ Romans 8:15

Anxiety

We feel anxious about what will happen next. What bad decision will our child make to further hurt himself/herself or others? The Word of God teaches us that in Christ we don't have to be anxious.

- ▶ Psalm 94:19
- ▶ Philippians 4:6
- ▶ 1 Peter 5:7

Shame

We are ashamed. We feel that others think that the way our child has become is our fault. Scripture tells us that if we look to Christ we will never be put to shame.

- ▶ Psalm 31:1b
- ▶ Psalm 34:5
- ▶ Romans 10:11b

Guilt

Guilt can crush us from inside, sapping the joy out of life and leaving us lonely, bitter and discouraged. Many of us have lived with guilt for so long that we don't allow ourselves to talk, trust or feel. When our child is making decisions that are negative and hurtful, we may fall into a state of despair. In Psalm 38:4 David cried out saying, "My guilt has overwhelmed me like a burden too heavy to bear." Guilt and shame are such significant reactions, that next week we will devote our entire discussion to these subjects.

- ▶ Psalm 38:4, 15
- ▶ Psalm 32:5

Emotions We Encounter

⤍ Activity

List the top three emotions that you are currently experiencing.
Share one of the emotions you listed.

1. _____

2. _____

3. _____

⤍ Moving Forward

ROLLER COASTER OF EMOTIONS
⤍ **Color in the descriptions with which you most identify.**

▸ How have these emotions stopped you from moving forward towards healing?

▸ Choose one or two of the Scriptures we read that spoke to you the most and write them down in your journal.

> *"The curriculum highlighted the roller-coaster of emotions we felt, validating our experience. As I heard other mothers share their struggles, prayer requests, heartaches and victories, I left encouraged."* – Dyanne

⤍ Closing Prayer

⤍ Preview of Next Week

GUILT, SHAME, CONVICTION, AND REPENTANCE – Next week we will be discussing guilt and shame and how we can move beyond them and forgive ourselves.

Roller Coaster of Emotions

Color in the emotions with which you most identify.

© Copyright Hurting Moms, Mending Hearts

How have these emotions stopped you from moving forward towards healing?

_____

_____

_____

_____

_____

_____

_____

_____

_____

_____

Moving Forward Journal

Choose one or two of the Scriptures we read that spoke to you and write them down.

_____

_____

_____

_____

_____

_____

_____

_____

_____

_____

What did these verses mean to you?

_____

_____

_____

_____

_____

_____

_____

_____

_____

_____

_____

_____

_____

Prayer Requests

Name: _____

Situation:_____

_____

_____

_____

_____

_____

Name: _____

Situation:_____

_____

_____

_____

_____

_____

Name: _____

Situation:_____

_____

_____

_____

_____

_____

Name: _____

Situation:_____

_____

_____

_____

_____

_____

SESSION FIVE
Guilt, Shame, Conviction, and Repentance

---→ Opening Prayer

---→ Key Scripture

"My guilt has overwhelmed me like a burden too heavy to bear. LORD, I wait for You; You will answer, Lord My God."
– Psalm 38:4, 15

---→ Sharing

Share one of the Scriptures you wrote about last week and tell how you related to it.

---→ Video

"I put my ministry at the church on hold in the past because of the guilt and shame that I was feeling. But through Hurting Moms, I am taking my life back!"
– Liz

Scan to see Video

---→ Discussion

Guilt, Shame, Conviction, and Repentance

Guilt

▸ Guilt is a feeling of responsibility or regret for a wrong or an offense. We experience guilt as a result of our actions, whether real or imagined. Guilt often leads to avoidance and can create dread, causing us to place responsibility for what has happened on someone else.

▸ We dwell on the past, the way which we have raised our children and the choices we have made. We feel we have added to the current situation in a substantial way. All of us can think of occasions when we blew it, when we made bad decisions, or when our indiscretions had some kind of an impact on our children. We feel remorse over these actions, but refuse to say, "I was wrong. Please forgive me." This is where the real problem occurs. The first part of change is to accept our part of the responsibility.

▸ Although we cannot go back in time, we long to be released from the guilt that weighs so heavily on us. Nowhere in Scripture does it say that if we had just done the right thing as parents, our child would be walking with God today. In fact, the Scriptures teach us that each person has a sinful nature and a free will. Romans 3:23 says, *"For all have sinned and fall short of the glory of God."* Look carefully at that verse again. It says ALL, not some, but ALL have sinned and fall short of the glory of God.

▸ Therefore, we must use both reason and faith to move beyond any oppressive guilt we feel to experience the joy of being forgiven and loved by God. We did the best we knew how to do and if we wronged our child, as most of us have in one way or another, we need to respond to the conviction of God's Spirit and experience His grace.

▸ Some of you may have a child who likes to remind you of the ways in which you failed him or her in the past. They are angry and bitter; they are not ready to accept responsibility for their own actions. They seem to take advantage of every opportunity to hurt you with their words. Once we are able to accept God's forgiveness and to forgive ourselves we can say to our child, "*That was then and this is now. I cannot go back and change the past, but I can be the best mom I know how to be to you today. I refuse to take responsibility for the choices you are making.*" There is complete freedom, not only being able to say those words, but to believe them!

Shame

▸ Shame can arise as we become aware of our guilt, but it is not the same thing as guilt. It is a painful feeling concerning how we appear to others and it doesn't always mean that we have done something wrong.

▸ Where guilt can happen as a result of offending or hurting someone else, shame is more an inward reflection of ourselves. It manifests itself with painful feelings of embarrassment, disgrace. We feel like we are the only ones who are struggling with a child who is out of control and we want to hide because we are ashamed.

▸ Shame tells us that we are undeserving of anything good and it neither encourages us nor gives us the desire or motivation to change our behavior.

▸ We must remember that God has feelings too. Jesus wept at the death of his dear friend Lazarus. (John 11:35) He feels much the same as we do, especially when we are hurting, or have stepped outside of His plan for our lives and are lost. We need to let God come close and share in our pain. He knows our hearts and our minds and He empathizes with us over our children, who are also His children. We need to allow His presence to reassure and strengthen us.

▸ While God is prepared to support us in our pain, He does not intend for us to remain locked into it indefinitely. He has something better for us. But first we need to face our shame head on, and deal with the deep feelings we have buried.

SCRIPTURE TELLS US OVER AND OVER AGAIN THAT THROUGH JESUS WE NO LONGER HAVE TO LIVE IN SHAME.

"*Anyone who trusts in Him will never be put to shame.*" – Romans 10:11b

"*Those who look to Him are radiant; their faces are never covered with shame.*" – Psalm 34:5

"*Do not be afraid; you will not be put to shame. Do not fear disgrace; you will not be humiliated. You will forget the shame of your youth and remember no more the reproach of your widowhood.*" – Isaiah 54:4

Conviction

▸ Conviction tells us our behavior is wrong. We become convicted when we begin to focus on God's opinion of us. We realize that He loves us and we want to please Him. Whereas guilt and shame do not bring "action", conviction produces action without the feelings of worthlessness. It leads us to repentance, forgiveness, and refreshment, so we no longer feel compelled to blame anyone else.

▸ As we examine our guilt and shame we begin to be convicted that our actions or attitudes have contributed to the problems with our child. The conviction we are experiencing gives us courage to approach those we have hurt to restore the relationship. At this time we put aside the pain that has been caused to us, and focus on making amends for the hurt or damage we may have caused. Once we face and acknowledge our part, we begin to experience the beginning of freedom.

"*Do to others as you would have them do to you.*" – Luke 6:31

"*Do nothing out of selfish ambition or vain conceit. Rather, in humility value others above your self, not looking to your own interests but each of you to the interests of the others.*" – Philippians 2:3-4

Repentance

▸ How do we discover the peace that comes from knowing that God has forgiven us? God can and will free us from guilt and shame. In fact, He wants to do just that, but first we need to repent in order to be forgiven.

▸ Repentance means to turn away from sin and turn toward God. Once we have honestly and sincerely confessed our sin and repented, or have turned away from it, we will finally start to experience the peace and the joy we have needed for so long. God is amazingly patient with us when we are honest with Him. Because Jesus died on the cross for our sins, God's mercy and grace flow freely to us when we truly confess and repent.

CONSIDER THE FOLLOWING SCRIPTURES:

"Then I acknowledged my sin to You and did not cover up my iniquity. I said, 'I will confess my transgressions to the Lord.' And You forgave the guilt of my sin." – Psalm 32:5

"Therefore, my friends, I want you to know that through Jesus the forgiveness of sins is proclaimed to you." – Acts 13:38

"Repentance for the forgiveness of sins will be preached in His name to all nations." – Luke 24:47a

"Yet now I am happy, not because you were made sorry, but because your sorrow led you to repentance." – 2 Corinthians 7:9

"I have not come to call the righteous, but sinners to repentance" – Luke 5:32

▸ By repenting we get rid of this excess baggage that continually weighs us down, and we can move on to see our lives be used by God to make a positive spiritual impact on our children.

▸ A wonderful verse to meditate on in closing is Ezekiel 18:20b, *"The son will not share the guilt of the parent, nor will the parent share the guilt of the son. The righteousness of the righteous will be credited to them, and the wickedness of the wicked will be charged against them."*

Guilt, Shame, Conviction, and Repentance

---> ## Activity

List 5 things that you have done well as a parent.
Share at least one of these things with the group.

---> ## Moving Forward

Write a prayer of repentance to God. Include specific things you are sorry for and ask for His forgiveness.

"When I wrote the letter I felt lighter. There was so much weight from the anxiety and fear that I had and it was lifted off of me. The cry that poured out of my heart to the Lord in prayer relieved me from the shame and guilt and reassured me that I was not a failing parent."
– Vickie

---> ## Closing Prayer

---> ## Preview of Next Week

HOW WE RESPOND TO OUR CHILD – Next week we will discuss the different ways in which we respond to our child.

Activity

List 5 things that you have done well as a parent.

1. _____

2. _____

3. _____

4. _____

5. _____

Write your prayer of repentance (a letter to God). Be sure to focus on your own behavior and NOT your child's behavior.

This letter is completely about you and what you want to say to God regarding the things for which you would like forgiveness. This letter is not about forgiveness from your child, but asking forgiveness from your Heavenly Father.

Come to group next week prepared to share your letter of repentance.

Sample Letter:

Dear God,

Forgive me for the times I was so wrapped up in my own relationships and I was so busy partying that I neglected my child. I acknowledge that I have many times been irresponsible as a parent and I am so sorry.

Going forward I choose to put You first in my life, following Your Word as my handbook for life. I know that with Your help, I will make better choices as a parent. Thank You for Your forgiveness, Your grace, and most of all for Your love.

In Jesus Name,
AMEN

SOME THINGS FROM WHICH YOU CAN REPENT

▸ Not paying attention to your child
▸ Your own addictions and hang-ups
▸ Being highly critical
▸ Being controlling
▸ Being too busy
▸ Not having proper boundaries
▸ Being co-dependent
▸ Being quick tempered
▸ Being out of control
▸ Exposing your child to an abusive spouse or relative
▸ Lacking in moral guidance
▸ Turning to food, drugs, work, sleep etc…as a way to cope, instead of to God

Repentance Letter

You can use this outline for your letter.

Dear God,
Please forgive me for

_____

_____

_____

_____

_____

_____

_____

_____

Going forward I choose to

_____

_____

_____

_____

_____

_____

_____

_____

Thank you that I am forgiven and

_____

_____

_____

Prayer Requests

Name: _____

Situation: _____

_____

_____

_____

_____

_____

Name: _____

Situation: _____

_____

_____

_____

_____

_____

Name: _____

Situation: _____

_____

_____

_____

_____

_____

Name: _____

Situation: _____

_____

_____

_____

_____

_____

SESSION SIX
How We Respond to Our Child

---▶ Opening Prayer

---▶ Key Scripture

"Instead, speaking the truth in love, we will grow to become in every respect the mature body of Him who is the head, that is, Christ."
– Ephesians 4:15

---▶ Sharing

Share our repentance letters to God. It may take some courage to do this, but it is very freeing to be able to share with others what we have written.

---▶ Video

" I came to a level of acceptance when I realized that God was in control and I wasn't. There was a complete burden lifted from my shoulders and it was freeing!" – Brenda

Scan to see Video

---▶ Discussion

We have talked about the emotions that we encounter as we become aware of our child's behavior. We have come to terms with our own guilt and shame and have acquired some tools for moving beyond them. But how are we responding to our problem children? What does the interaction between you and your child look like? Have you chosen to reject your child or are you confronting and correcting him or her with acceptance and encouragement?

Rejection

▸ One of the temptations that we have as parents is to reject our child who is out of control. Rejection is something we do in order to feel better or to mask the pain that we are experiencing due to the actions of our child. It helps us to feel we have "control" of something in the midst of the chaos. We can reject our child by dismissing or eliminating them from our lives by telling them to leave our home – kicking them out. We communicate that as long as they are doing what they are doing we do not want to have a relationship with them.

▸ This form of rejection is severe and narrows the chances for eventual reconciliation as the child feels as if they are no longer a member of the family. Please note here that there may be times that forcing our child to leave our home is part of setting healthy boundaries. In that case, telling him or her to move out should never be done in a moment of anger or rage. It should be done with a plan in place that has been agreed upon by both parents and communicated with the child in a way that expresses love and concern for them, yet conveys an intolerance of their behavior.

▸ There is another form of rejection which is much more subtle and definitely less direct: ignoring or refusing to consider the child. Although rejecting someone in this way is more passive, it is definitely noticeable and causes a tremendous amount of tension in the home as it can drag on for weeks, months, or even years, affecting the entire family in a negative way. Unfortunately, this form of rejection is one that many parents employ.

▸ It is highly unlikely that our child will come around or change because we reject them. In fact, rejection creates a barrier that can push our child further away and it does not help us move in the direction of resolving any of the issues that are causing the problems or the distance between us.

▸ In order for us to reconcile and restore our relationship with our child there are several things that need to happen. We have to confront them for the purpose of correcting them, and at the same time we must convey our acceptance and give them encouragement.

Confrontation

▸ The first step in the healing of any relationship is to approach or confront the person, in this case our child, in order to communicate our feelings. We confront our child, not to fight with them, but to express our love for them. If we don't care about someone, we don't spend the time or energy confronting them about their behavior.

▸ Confronting our child includes letting them know that we are aware of what is going on with them. This will most likely be painful for one or both of us. It may mean that we have to place restrictions on them if they live in our home or that we may have to ask them to move out of our home altogether. This could mean cutting them off financially. Confronting our child involves giving them consequences if their undesirable behavior continues. However, it is the manner in which we confront our child that will determine whether or not they will be open to engaging in a dialog with us at all.

THE BIBLE GIVES US GUIDELINES FOR CONFRONTING:

> *"Better is open rebuke than hidden love."* – Proverbs 27:5
> *"Those whom I love I rebuke and discipline."* – Revelation 3:19

As we consider approaching or confronting our child there are some important guidelines to keep in mind.

▸ **Be honest**
Don't try to beat around the bush or sugar coat what you are saying, but strive to "speak the truth in love".

> *"Therefore each of you must put off falsehood and speak truthfully."* – Ephesians 4:25a

▸ **Be gentle**
All people, including your child, respond best to expressions of care and concern.

> *"A gentle answer turns away wrath, but a harsh word stirs up anger."* – Proverbs 15:1

▸ **Be vulnerable**
If we keep our defenses down and stay open to hearing what our child has to say, even though it may be hurtful, it will help to keep the doors of communication open and promote productivity.

▸ **Be realistic**
If we are realistic we will not be overwhelmed and controlled by our feelings and we won't be disappointed by unrealistic expectations.

Acceptance

▸ Acceptance is the opposite of rejection. We may not approve of what our child is doing or the way in which they are living, but if they feel accepted it will help to bridge the gap and soften their hearts. Rejection will result in resistance and the shutting down of communication, but acceptance will encourage openness and willingness to listen.

▸ Remember, we are not accepting their behavior, but we are accepting them as our child; a valued member of our family, who we have loved since before they were born. We may be powerless to feel acceptance at this point, but if we rely on Christ's strength and love we will begin to see them as He sees them. This will help us to accept them for who they are in spite of all of the drama, turmoil, chaos, and pain.

Encouragement

▸ One of the ways we can show that we accept our child is by encouraging them. If our attitude is hopeful, cheerful and positive, and we speak and act with confidence, it will encourage them to be more relational and we will have a better chance of having positive interactions with them. If we can find one positive thing to affirm in them each day, they are bound to respond with something positive of their own eventually.

▸ Encouragement should be given kindly, generously and with no attached conditions; in other words, without expecting anything in return. In order to do this we must, again, depend on the strength and love of Jesus to help us with patience and consistency.

"Therefore encourage one another and build each other up, just as in fact you are doing."
– 1 Thessalonians 5:11

"But encourage one another daily, as long as it is called 'Today', so that none of you may be hardened by sin's deceitfulness." – Hebrews 3:13

"Let us not neglect our meeting together, as some people do, but encourage one another, especially now that the day of His return is drawing near." – Hebrews 10:25 (NLT)

How We Respond to Our Child

➔ Activities

Which of these responses have you had with your child?
Why do you think it was effective or not effective?

➔ Moving Forward

▸ Write 10 positive things about your child.

▸ List 3 ways you can encourage your child this week (if they are within reach).

▸ Write a letter to your child that demonstrates your acceptance by encouraging them. Use the tools we have discussed. Be prepared to share your letter with the group next week.

▸ Optional – Read or send your letter to your child

> "When given the assignment of trying to remember positive things about my child I wasn't looking forward to it. When I sat down ready to start I must have stared at the paper for an hour. It was hard. I had to take off my anger and hurt blinders. It had been a long time since I thought anything positive about my son, everything was negative.
>
> I started to remember when he was little...riding a tricycle for the first time, playing roller hockey, his beautiful drawings...as I began to write those memories down others came to mind and then more, certain things we had done together, long ago.
>
> It was a painful journey to see how many things I had forgotten that were wonderful about my son. It gave my heart the feeling it needed. I needed to remember and be hopeful that God is in control and to hold onto the love I have for all the good things about my child.
>
> *"Writing the first positive thing was the toughest, and then it got easier!"* – Michelle

➔ Closing Prayer

➔ Preview of Next Week

LETTING GO OF OUR CHILD – Next week we will be discussing how we can let go of our child and trust them in the hands of God. There is a freedom that comes from letting go. By doing this, we feel that we have our life back again.

Moving Forward Activity

Write 10 positive things about your child.

1. _____

2. _____

3. _____

4. _____

5. _____

6. _____

7. _____

8. _____

9. _____

10. _____

List 3 ways you can encourage your child this week (if they are within reach).
Keep in mind that their reaction doesn't matter. It's only what you do that matters.

1. _____

2. _____

3. _____

Moving Forward Journal

Write a letter to your child that demonstrates your acceptance by encouraging them. Use the tools we have discussed tonight. Be prepared to share your letter with the group next week.

Dear _____,

_____

_____

_____

_____

_____

_____

_____

_____

_____

_____

_____

_____

_____

_____

_____

_____

_____

_____

_____

_____

_____

_____

Prayer Requests

Name: _____

Situation: _____

_____

_____

_____

_____

_____

Name: _____

Situation: _____

_____

_____

_____

_____

_____

Name: _____

Situation: _____

_____

_____

_____

_____

_____

Name: _____

Situation: _____

_____

_____

_____

_____

_____

SESSION SEVEN
Letting Go of Our Child

---> Opening Prayer

---> Key Scripture

"I prayed for this child, and the Lord has granted me what I asked of him. So now I give him to the Lord. For his whole life he will be given over to the Lord." – 1 Samuel 1:27-28a

---> Sharing

Share the letters of encouragement that we wrote during the week with the rest of the group.

How did writing this letter make us feel?

---> Video

"Letting go and letting God is extremely difficult, but once you are able to completely let go, even if it is for a short period of time, you feel peaceful knowing that your child is safe and that God will take care of them. You have a peace that allows you to carry on with your life!"
– Teri

---> Discussion

Scan to see Video

---→ **Activity**

Read Luke 15:11-32.

Most of us know the story of the Prodigal Son. The father in this story is a wonderful example of a parent who "let go" of his child. This dad loved his son and he knew his boy would make bad choices if he left. But the dad didn't try to control his son by refusing to give him his inheritance. He gave it to him and allowed him to go and to make his own mistakes. Letting him go and allowing him to squander all of this money so that he ended up eating with the pigs was exactly what that young man needed in order to realize that what he had wasn't so bad after all. He went home and asked his father for forgiveness. That would never have happened if that dad had not let go of his son.

Things We Believe

▶ As parents, many of us believe that we have power or control over our children. We see our child as someone we are to shape and conform in to who we think they should be. In our own minds, our desires, ideas and viewpoints are what matter most in life so we try to implant these in our children.

▶ Some of us think that our adult children should still answer to us. It is hard to let go after all the years of comforting, supporting and directing them in the manner in which we thought they should be raised.

▶ Whether our child is still in our home or out on their own, we feel that they should be obligated to us and thankful for all we have done for them over the years. We are disappointed and hurt when this doesn't happen. Let's not forget the pleasure we have had in providing for them and find a way to be content. If we don't we will be allowing our child to control our happiness and sense of well-being.

▶ Most of us thought that our family would always have a strong bond.

▶ It may be difficult to understand that our children have to find their own way of living because we have always assumed that they would live by our standards.

Why We Hold On

▶ Being a mom is such a huge part of who we are that releasing our children may seem impossible. This loss feels like the end of life as we have known it.

▶ We have begun to realize that we cannot control our child. Our efforts at trying to fix them haven't worked, but if we let go of them we feel like we have failed as a parent.

▶ Letting go of our child means that we are unable to safeguard or shield them from harm. The reality is that the harm is being caused by their own choices and although we have tried, there is nothing we can do about it.

Letting Go of Our Child

Our Roles As Moms

As a mom, we have been responsible for caring for our family for so long. When our children become adults we want to hang on to them a little longer than we should. So many times our good intentions are actually detrimental to our child, our family, and especially to ourselves. Let's look at some of the unhealthy ways in which we often try to hold on to our adult children.

▸ *Sacrificing* – We lose ourselves by constantly putting others first. This is more damaging than it seems. It shelters our children from reality and slows down their development.

▸ *Savior* – We cannot save or protect them. We often feel guilty if we know our child needs help and refuses to engage in getting help for themselves. We feel that it is still our responsibility to make them better. Our actions or attitudes can be the very things that get in the way of some thing God is trying to do in the life of our child. We are not the "savior" – He is.

▸ *Selfishness* – Our emphasis is on how we are being made to feel by the actions of our child and not on what is actually going on with them. We still want to regulate them by trying to make them feel guilty about not being thankful for all we have done for them. We are afraid that if we separate ourselves from our child we won't be needed any longer.

Surrendering Our Kids

Surrendering does not mean that we give up on our child. If we give up on someone, we abandon them. Surrendering means that we let go and give our child the freedom to make mistakes, but we also allow them to pay the consequences for those mistakes.

When we surrender our children:

▸ We stop being accountable for them, but we still follow through on our obligations to them.

▸ We trust God more and we rely less on what our child is doing or not doing for our sense of well-being.

▸ We become free from the emotional roller-coaster ride, because our emotional state is no longer reliant on our child's actions.

▸ We give our child the independence they need so they can be motivated by God instead of by our nagging, meddling or manipulation.

▸ We begin to see that we are not responsible for the choices our child makes, which reduces the guilt we have been experiencing.

Disengaging From Our Kids

▸ We never separate from our child, but we disengage ourselves from their problematic behavior.

▸ Disengagement happens when we begin to recognize our child as a distinct and detached being.

▸ Disengagement is important if we are to overcome the negative emotions that have been destroying us. It is also important because our child must begin to develop their individuality.

▸ We must choose to disengage from our child. However difficult this may be, it won't happen unless we make a deliberate decision to do so.

▸ Remember, relinquishment is giving someone up, but abandonment is giving up on someone. We are NOT abandoning our kids by disengaging from them or letting go of them.

----▸ Activity

Read the Letting Go poem.

▸ Each mom reads two lines of the poem aloud.

▸ Discuss ways in which we can let go.

----▸ Moving Forward

▸ Choose one or more things in the poem that resonate with you.

▸ Write about it and be prepared to share it next week.

▸ Do something for YOU this week!

> *"The Letting Go poem showed me that my situation is out of my control. I've totally given my son to the Lord. My focus now is to ask God to give me strength and move mightily in my life. I feel free!"* – Adrienne

→ Closing Prayer

→ Preview of Next Week

PRAYING FOR OUR CHILD – Next week we will be discussing ways in which we can pray for our child.

Letting Go

To let go doesn't mean to stop caring,
It means I can't do it for someone else.

To let go is not to cut myself off,
It's the realization that I can't control another.

To let go is not to enable,
But to allow learning from natural consequences.

To let go is to admit powerlessness,
Which means the outcome is not in my hands.

To let go is not to try to change or blame another,
I can only change myself.

To let go is not to fix,
But to be supportive.

To let go is not to judge,
But to allow another to be a human being.

To let go is not to be in the middle arranging all the outcomes,
But to allow others to effect their own outcomes.

To let go is not to be protective,
It is to permit another to face reality.

To let go is not to deny,
But to accept.

To let go is not to nag, scold, or argue,
But to search out my own shortcomings and to correct them.

To let go is not to adjust everything to my desires,
But to take each day as it comes.

To let go is not to criticize and regulate anyone,
But to try to become what dream I can be.

To let go is not to regret the past,
But to grow and live for the future.

To let go is to fear less and love more!

Author Unknown

Moving Forward Journal

Choose one or more things in the poem that resonate with you.

_____

_____

_____

_____

_____

_____

_____

_____

_____

_____

Do something just for you this week! Make it memorable. It should be something that you really enjoy, something that you have not been able to do in a long time for yourself.

List some ideas for things that you can do for yourself this week and commit to doing at least one of them.

1. _____

2. _____

3. _____

4. _____

5. _____

Prayer Requests

Name: _____

Situation: _____

_____

_____

_____

_____

_____

Name: _____

Situation: _____

_____

_____

_____

_____

_____

Name: _____

Situation: _____

_____

_____

_____

_____

_____

Name: _____

Situation: _____

_____

_____

_____

_____

_____

SESSION EIGHT
Praying for Our Child

·····➤ Opening Prayer

·····➤ Key Scripture

"Arise, cry out in the night, as the watches of the night begin; pour out your heart like water in the presence of the Lord. Lift up your hands to Him for the lives of your children, who faint from hunger at every street corner." – Lamentations 2:19

·····➤ Sharing

▸ Share insights from Letting Go poem.
▸ What did you do for YOU this week?

·····➤ Video

"Sometimes you are the only one that is standing in the gap for your child, but it takes a group of people to be able to pray and intercede. You're standing in the gap for your loved one because they can't." – Trenda

Scan to see Video

·····➤ Discussion

73

Thoughts About Prayer

▶ Before we can consider how and what to pray for, we need to remember what we have learned. Children do not really belong to us. They are not our possessions. We must take the first step and give our child back to God. We have to turn them and their lifestyle over to the Lord.

▶ In order to come to God with our fears, worries, and requests we must come with humility. We are basically telling Him that we need Him and that we recognize our own powerlessness in our situation. We are coming with a willingness to surrender any control we think we have and to totally submit to his will.

▶ When we pray or talk to God it opens us up to his unconditional peace even in the midst of our turmoil. It also invites him to be present in the lives of those for whom we pray. Something always happens when we pray and we can be certain that when we "stand in the gap" for our child, God hears our prayers and his power will bring about change.

> *"God will grant them repentance leading them to a knowledge of the truth and that they will come to their senses and escape from the trap of the devil, who has taken them captive to do His will."* – 2 Timothy 2:25b-26

> *"Pray without ceasing."* – 1 Thessalonians 5:17

What to Pray

▶ Pray that your child will be shielded from any emotional, physical and mental damage.
▶ Pray that they will experience God's presence in the midst of where they are and what they are doing.
▶ Pray that they will see themselves as one who is valued and loved.
▶ Pray they will have strength to say no to temptations and to endure the hardships they may encounter.
▶ Pray that they will change direction and leave the destructive path they are on.
▶ Pray for the people around them and for their friendships.
▶ Pray for them to never forget that you love them.
▶ Praise God for your child, for who they are and who they will grow to be.

Praying the Scriptures Over Our Child

Use passages of Scripture to formulate prayers or say the verses back to God and make them our own petitions. Saying them aloud each day will encourage and strengthen us.

▸ Helps us to avoid becoming stuck in a rut.
▸ Helps us to organize and to define what we want to say.
▸ Gives us confidence and a sense of expectancy.
▸ Helps us grow in our own personal relationship with the Lord.
▸ Opens us up to the work of the Holy Spirit and what He can do in and through us.

┅➤ Activity

▸ Share some of the ways you are currently praying for your child.
▸ Circle some of the new ways that you would like to start praying for your child.

▸ Read the poem "A Mending Heart".
  ▸ Each mom, in turn, reads two lines of the poem aloud.
  ▸ Discuss anything that stood out to you in the poem.

┅➤ Moving Forward

▸ Choose two Scriptures that you want to use in praying for your child.
▸ Write a sample prayer that you will pray aloud for your child each morning.
▸ Use the sample prayers below to help get you started along with the Scriptures provided at the back of the book or the HMMH Scripture Cards.

> "It is my daily time in Scripture that keeps me from falling apart. I stand on Psalm 41:2 and personalize it by saying, '*I have His promises that give me hope, knowing He will preserve my kids. He will keep them alive and bless them among the earth. He will not surrender them to the will of their enemies.*'" – Joanne

┅➤ Closing Prayer

┅➤ Preview of Next Week

WHAT HAVE WE LEARNED? – Next week we will discuss what we have learned during our time together for the past eight weeks. Be thinking about some of the ways in which participating in the group has helped you in your journey as a **Hurting Mom**. How has your heart begun to mend?

A Mending Heart

I came to God
  bruised and battered.
My heart is still broken...
  Did it even matter?

My kid is on the street
  and O' what a mess.
My heart is broken...
  Is he homeless?

Checking social media
  looking for his face.
My heart is still hurting...
  He is gone without a trace.

He wounded me deeply
  this is so unfair.
My heart is hurting...
  Did he even care?

Letting go and giving him up
  to authorities and such.
My heart is still aching...
  Did I give him enough?

Releasing him to God
  through all my suffering.
My heart is aching...
  Did I do the right thing?

I don't have to stay
  in this devastating place.
My heart is still mending...
  as I wait to see his face.

A weight has come off
  as I release it to Thee.
My heart is mending...
  I'm beginning to break free!

My sobbing and hurting
  is coming to an end.
My heart is still healing...
  I'm beginning to mend.

It started with hurting
  but with God's great love.
My heart is mending...
  with stitches from above.

I trust You with my child's heart
  and all You can do.
His heart You are mending...
  as he comes back to You!

Sherry Lynn Ward

Moving Forward Journal

⸱⸱⸱→ Choose two Scriptures provided at the back of the book.
⸱⸱⸱→ Write a prayer that you will pray aloud for your child each morning.

Sample Prayer 1

Thank you, Lord, that You know the plans You have for _____, to prosper and not harm them, but to give them a hope and a future. I pray that my child will not stand in the way of sinners or sit in the seat of mockers. May my child's delight be in the law of the Lord as they meditate on it day and night. (Jeremiah 29:11, Psalm 1:1, 2)

Sample Prayer 2

Dear Father, may _____, like your Son, grow in wisdom and stature, and in favor with You and the people his life touches. Give him a listening ear to parental instructions. Help him to pay attention that he may gain understanding. (Luke 2:52; Proverbs 4:1)

Lord,
Thank you for _____,
Thank you that the Your Word says...

_____

_____

_____

_____

_____

_____

_____

_____

_____

_____

Prayer Requests

Name: _____

Situation: _____

_____

_____

_____

_____

_____

Name: _____

Situation: _____

_____

_____

_____

_____

_____

Name: _____

Situation: _____

_____

_____

_____

_____

_____

Name: _____

Situation: _____

_____

_____

_____

_____

_____

SESSION NINE
What Have We Learned

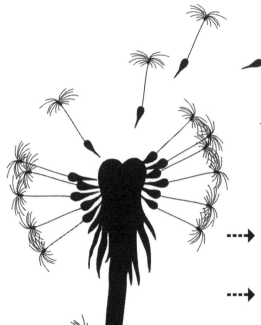

----▶ Opening Prayer

----▶ Key Scripture

"And the God of all grace, who called you to His eternal glory in Christ, after you have suffered a little while, will Himself restore you and make you strong, firm, and steadfast." – I Peter 5:10

----▶ Sharing

Read aloud the prayers that we have written for our children during the week.

----▶ Video

*"**Hurting Moms** has showed me I'm not alone. There are women going through the same thing I am going through."* – Rhonda

Scan to see Video

----▶ Discussion

83

What Have We Learned?

Tonight marks our ninth week together as **Hurting Moms**. By sharing this journey we have discovered that we are not alone. We have been able to identify the various phases and emotions that we experience as moms when our child is out of control or estranged from us. We have learned to respond to our child in a way that is healthy rather than in a damaging way. We have been given tools for releasing our child to God and discovered ways of praying for them. Most importantly, we have learned to trust and rely on God, who loves our children more than we do and wants us to live with peace and joy instead of the pain brought on by our disappointment, anger, fear, guilt, and shame.

This week we are going to look back and see the progress we have made as we have moved toward freedom through sharing with one another and by utilizing the tools we have been given.

----▶ Activity

Using a scale of 0 to 5 (0 meaning "not at all" and 5 meaning "significant achievement") how would you rate yourself in each of the following?

1. I am giving up my need/desire to control my child. _____

2. I am trusting God, but I'm not giving up on my child. _____

3. I am dealing with the disappointments. _____

4. I am working through the phases and learning to recognize my emotions. _____

5. I can see my child's misery as the result of his/her choices. _____

6. I am honoring my child's freedom of choice. _____

7. I am facing the possibility that my relationship with my child may never be
   what I wish it could be. _____

8. I am accepting the fact that I don't always have to understand. _____

9. I am beginning to experience peace and joy in my life again. _____

Quick Share

Let's all share our response to one or two of the questions above.

Planning A Celebration Together

Plan a potluck for next week. Plan to meet at one of the participant's home, if possible. Make it special.

What Have We Learned

····→ Moving Forward

Reflect on how this group has helped you in moving forward in your journey towards a mending heart.

What are some things you'd still like to work on that you have learned in this group?

> "At the end of every meeting I went home uplifted and I felt I had regained some strength to fight those difficult battles. As the weeks progressed, I noticed that I was speaking differently and for the first time in many months I could have a conversation with my son without getting into an argument. If the conversation was not going well, I was able to stop it before it got out of hand." – Fabiola

····→ Closing Prayer

····→ Preview of Next Week

CELEBRATION – Next week we will be celebrating how far we have come and we will be speaking a blessing for our children.

Planning A Celebration

Date: _____

Time: _____

Where: _____

What we will bring to share: _____

NAME _____ BRINGING _____

_____ _____

_____ _____

_____ _____

_____ _____

_____ _____

_____ _____

_____ _____

_____ _____

_____ _____

_____ _____

_____ _____

_____ _____

Moving Forward Journal

Reflect on how this group has helped you in moving forward in your journey towards a mending heart.

_____

_____

_____

_____

_____

_____

_____

_____

_____

What are some things you'd still like to work on that you have learned in the group?

_____

_____

_____

_____

_____

_____

_____

_____

_____

_____

_____

_____

Prayer Requests

Name: _____

Situation: _____

_____

_____

_____

_____

_____

Name: _____

Situation: _____

_____

_____

_____

_____

_____

Name: _____

Situation: _____

_____

_____

_____

_____

_____

Name: _____

Situation: _____

_____

_____

_____

_____

_____

SESSION TEN
Celebration

┈┈▶ Opening Prayer

┈┈▶ Key Scripture

"They celebrate Your abundant goodness and joyfully sing of Your righteousness." – Psalm 145:7

┈┈▶ Sharing A Meal Together

Tonight we celebrate, not necessarily because our kids are better or back on track, but because we are learning how to have joy even in the midst of the process. God's goodness is abundant and we know how to seek comfort and wisdom from the Scriptures now. As we continue to lift up our children in prayer, we are able to release them knowing that our heavenly Father sees them and loves them.

┈┈▶ Video

"God has your kids in the palm of His hand and He's not going to let them go. God loves these kids. God has something very special in mind for your child."
– Sis Conley

Scan to see Video

┈┈▶ Discussion

93

Celebration

---→ Discussion

We have developed close, loving, and trusting relationships through this group. I want to encourage you to continue to pray for one another and to hold each other accountable in using the tools we have learned.

God has definitely shown up in our group. He has been with us week after week as we have looked to Him for our healing. We can take comfort in knowing that His promises are real and we can confidently put our trust in Him as we allow Him to lead us on this journey of being a parent.

---→ Activity

···→   Look at **"What's Next"** and circle two things you would like to do next.

What's Next?

Options

Circle two things you'd like to do next.

      1) Read one of the resource books that are suggested on the following page

        or at *www.HurtingMoms.com*.

        Which ones(s)?_____

        _____

      2) Repeat **Hurting Moms, Mending Hearts – Breaking Free**

      3) Sign up for the next level of the **Hurting Moms, Mending Hearts** group.

      4) Join a study group at your local church

      5) Join a Celebrate Recovery (CR) group in your area

⟶ ***Share with the group what you have committed to do next in your healing process.***

⟶ Moving Forward

Think about ways you are recognizing God working in your life since joining the group. Write about it.

    *"God has been so good to me through the **Hurting Moms, Mending Hearts** group. Shame, guilt, fear, hurt, and frustration were the many feelings that consumed me everyday as I dealt with my son's issues. Through **Hurting Moms**, I began a blessed journey of healing, hope, thankfulness, and yes, even joy! Even my marriage is in a better place. Through being able to open up and share with other women, I didn't feel like I was the only one. Through the love of God, He has shifted my feelings and heart to trust Him completely!" – Brenda*

⟶ Closing Prayer

Website

www.HurtingMoms.com

Email

info@HurtingMoms.com

FREE Daily encouraging words for Hurting Moms.

Cathy Taylor has put together words of encouragement using some of the Scriptures that have inspired her along her journey as a Hurting Mom. She hopes that they will bring you comfort and peace as you go through your day.

Sign up at *www.HurtingMoms.com*

Recommended Reading

▸ *A Journey Out of the Wilderness* by Sherry Lynn Ward

▸ *Closing the Door, but not my Heart* by Trenda Lineback

▸ *Daring Greatly* by Brené Brown

▸ *Praying for Your Adult Children* by Stormie Omartian

Recommended Websites

▸ www.BlueLetterBible.org – For Bible verses and original language

▸ www.SquareTreePublishing.com

Think about ways you are recognizing God working in your life since joining the group. Write about it.

Prayer Requests

Name: _____

Situation: _____

_____

_____

_____

_____

_____

Name: _____

Situation: _____

_____

_____

_____

_____

_____

Name: _____

Situation: _____

_____

_____

_____

_____

_____

Name: _____

Situation: _____

_____

_____

_____

_____

_____

Mending A Heart

Pray

It can be helpful to write out our prayers as if we are writing a letter to God. This prevents our minds from wandering as we pray and helps us to stay focused on the things that we want to talk to Him about. It also may be helpful for you to pray aloud. You could pray in the car as you are driving, or in the shower or while on a walk, whatever works for you. Let your feelings flow as you pray, remembering that prayer is simply talking to God. It doesn't have to be fancy – just speak or write from your heart.

Worship

Worship can be expressed in many ways such as: singing, dancing, or spending time in nature meditating on the goodness of God. Worshipping softens our hearts and opens us up to experiencing God's presence. When we worship we need to put everything else aside and simply focus on praising God. Even in the midst of sadness and pain we can find things to be grateful for, and it is important to think about those things and to express our thanks to Him. Find a place where you can be free to worship uninhibitedly, whether it is in your bedroom, in your car, or at the beach or park, etc.

Read Scripture

The Bible is our handbook for life and it is full of promises from God. Reading the Bible will comfort and sustain us and it will give us direction for handling and responding to every situation. When we open our Bible we allow the words of Scripture to penetrate our hearts. This draws us closer to God and we begin to experience peace, joy, and hope. When you discover a verse or a passage that speaks to you, read it over and over again, memorize it, journal about it. When it comes to reading the Bible, don't just skim over it, take time to dig in deep. As time goes on, the more you read the Bible, the better you will understand God and how great His love is towards you and your child.

Journal

Journaling is a great way to express our feelings. It helps us to organize and unload our thoughts. When our head is filled with so many cares, especially negative or painful thoughts, we can find release and relief by writing them down. Journaling our prayers and important verses or passages of Scripture enable us to see what God is doing in our lives.

Email Sign-up

Sign up for the **Hurting Moms, Mending Hearts** daily email. These daily boosts of encouragement will help you to stay positive and strong throughout the day.

Hurting Moms, Mending Hearts Group List

NAME	PHONE #	EMAIL

Scriptures for Encouragement

Session 1

"*Praise be to the God and Father of our Lord Jesus Christ, the Father of compassion and the God of all comfort, who comforts us in all our troubles, so that we can comfort those in any trouble with the comfort we ourselves receive from God.*" – 2 Corinthians 1:3-4

The Lord, "*heals the brokenhearted and binds up their wounds.*" – Psalm 147:3b

"*The God of all grace, who called you to His eternal glory in Christ, after you have suffered a little while, will Himself restore you and make you strong, firm and steadfast.*" – 1 Peter 5:10

"*Cast all your anxiety on Him because He cares for you.*"– 1 Peter 5:7

"*Do not fear, for I am with you; do not be dismayed, for I am your God. I will strengthen you and help you; I will uphold you with My righteous right hand,*" says the Lord. – Isaiah 41:10

Jesus said, "*Peace I leave with you; My peace I give you. I do not give to you as the world gives. Do not let your hearts be troubled and do not be afraid.*" – John 14:27

"*Be strong and courageous. Do not be terrified; do not be discouraged, for the Lord your God will be with you wherever you go,*" says the Lord. – Joshua 1:9b

Session 2

"*We wait in hope for the LORD: He is our help and our shield.*" – Psalm 33:20

Session 3

"*See, I am doing a new thing! Now it springs up; do you not perceive it?*" – Isaiah 43:19a

Session 4

"*All Scripture is God-breathed and is useful for teaching, rebuking, correcting and training in righteousness so that the servant of God may be thoroughly equipped for every good work.*" – 2 Timothy 3:16, 17

"*Praise be to the Lord, to God our savior, who daily bears our burdens.*" – Psalm 68:19

Jesus said, "*Come to me, all you who are weary and burdened, and I will give you rest.*" – Matthew 11:28

Scriptures for Encouragement

Disappointment

"And this hope will not lead to disappointment. For we know how dearly God loves us, because He has given us the Holy Spirit to fill our hearts with His love." – Romans 5:5 (NLT)

"My flesh and my heart may fail, but God is the strength of my heart and my portion forever." – Psalm 73:26

"You will know that I am the LORD; those who hope in Me will not be disappointed." – Isaiah 49:23b

Anger

"Refrain from anger and turn from wrath; do not fret – it leads only to evil." – Psalm 37:8

"Fools give full vent to their rage, but the wise bring calm in the end." – Proverbs 29:11

"In your anger do not sin. Do not let the sun go down while you are still angry." – Ephesians 4:26

"But now you must also rid yourselves of all such things as these: anger, rage, malice, slander, and filthy language from your lips." – Colossians 3:8

"Everyone should be quick to listen, slow to speak and slow to become angry, because human anger does not produce the righteousness that God desires." – James 1:19-20

Hurt

"He heals the brokenhearted and binds up their wounds." – Psalms 147:3

"But as for me, afflicted and in pain – may Your salvation, God, protect me." – Psalm 69:29

"My comfort in my suffering is this: Your promise preserves my life." – Psalm 119:50

"Bless those who curse you, pray for those who mistreat you." – Luke 6:28

Discouraged

"The LORD himself goes before you and will be with you; He will never leave you nor forsake you. Do not be afraid; do not be discouraged." – Deuteronomy 31:8

"Have I not commanded you? Be strong and courageous. Do not be afraid; do not be discouraged, for the LORD your God will be with you wherever you go." – Joshua 1:9

"Why, my soul, are you downcast? Why so disturbed within me? Put your hope in God, for I will yet praise Him, my Savior and my God." – Psalm 42:5

Scriptures for Encouragement

Fear

"*The LORD is my light and my salvation – whom shall I fear? The LORD is the stronghold of my life – of whom shall I be afraid?*" – Psalm 27:1

"*I sought the Lord, and He answered me; He delivered me from all my fears.*" – Psalm 34:4

"*When I am afraid, I put my trust in You.*" – Psalm 56:3

"*The Spirit you received does not make you slaves, so that you live in fear again; rather, the Spirit you received brought about your adoption to sonship. And by Him we cry, 'Abba, Father.'*" – Romans 8:15

Anxiety

"*When anxiety was great within me, Your consolation brought me joy.*" – Psalm 94:19

"*Do not be anxious about anything, but in every situation, by prayer and petition, with thanksgiving, present your requests to God.*" – Philippians 4:6

"*Cast all your anxiety on Him because He cares for you.*" – I Peter 5:7

Shame

"*In You, LORD, I have taken refuge; let me never be put to shame; deliver me in Your righteousness.*" – Psalm 31:1b

"*Those who look to Him are radiant; their faces are never covered with shame.*" – Psalm 34:5

"*Anyone who believes in Him will never be put to shame.*" – Romans 10:11b

Guilt

David cried out saying, "*My guilt has overwhelmed me like a burden too heavy to bear. LORD, I wait for You; You will answer, Lord My God.*" – Psalm 38:4, 15

Session 5

"My guilt has overwhelmed me like a burden too heavy to bear. LORD, I wait for You; You will answer, Lord My God." – Psalm 38:4, 15

Guilt

"For all have sinned and fall short of the glory of God." – Romans 3:23

Shame

"Jesus wept." – John 11:35

"Anyone who believes in Him will never be put to shame." – Romans 10:11b

"Those who look to Him are radiant; their faces are never covered with shame." – Psalm 34:5

"Do not be afraid; you will not be put to shame. Do not fear disgrace; you will not be humiliated. You will forget the shame of your youth and remember no more the reproach of your widowhood." – Isaiah 54:4

Conviction

"Do to others as you would have them do to you." – Luke 6:31

"Do nothing out of selfish ambition or vain conceit. Rather, in humility value others above yourself, not looking to your own interests but each of you to the interests of the others." – Philippians 2:3-4

Repentance

"Then I acknowledged my sin to You and did not cover up my iniquity. I said, 'I will confess my transgressions to the Lord.' And You forgave the guilt of my sin." – Psalm 32:5

"Therefore, my friends, I want you to know that through Jesus the forgiveness of sins is proclaimed to you." – Acts 13:38

"Repentance for the forgiveness of sins will be preached in His name to all nations." – Luke 24:47a

"Yet now I am happy, not because you were made sorry, but because your sorrow led you to repentance." – 2 Corinthians 7:9

"I have not come to call the righteous, but sinners to repentance" – Luke 5:32

"The son will not share the guilt of the parent, nor will the parent share the guilt of the son. The righteousness of the righteous will be credited to them, and the wickedness of the wicked will be charged against them." – Ezekiel 18:20b

Scriptures for Encouragement

Session 6

"Instead, speaking the truth in love, we will grow to become in every respect the mature body of Him who is the head, that is, Christ." – Ephesians 4:15

"Better is open rebuke than hidden love." – Proverbs 27:5

"Those whom I love I rebuke and discipline." – Revelation 3:19

"Therefore each of you must put off falsehood and speak truthfully." – Ephesians 4:25a

"A gentle answer turns away wrath, but a harsh word stirs up anger." – Proverbs 15:1

"Therefore encourage one another and build each other up, just as in fact you are doing." – 1 Thessalonians 5:11

"But encourage one another daily, as long as it is called, 'Today', so that none of you may be hardened by sin's deceitfulness." – Hebrews 3:13

"Let us not neglect our meeting together, as some people do, but encourage one another, especially now that the day of His return is drawing near." – Hebrews 10:25 (NLT)

Session 7

"I prayed for this child, and the Lord has granted me what I asked of him. So now I give him to the Lord. For his whole life he will be given over to the Lord." – 1 Samuel 1:27-28a

Prodigal Son – Luke 15:11-32

Session 8

"Arise, cry out in the night, as the watches of the night begin; pour out your heart like water in the presence of the Lord. Lift up your hands to Him for the lives of your children, who faint from hunger at every street corner." – Lamentations 2:19

"God will grant them repentance leading them to a knowledge of the truth and that they will come to their senses and escape from the trap of the devil, who has taken them captive to do His will." – 2 Timothy 2:25b-26

"Pray without ceasing." – 1 Thessalonians 5:17

"The LORD protects and preserves them – they are counted among the blessed in the land – He does not give them over to the desire of their foes." – Psalm 41:2

"'For I know the plans I have for you', declares the Lord, 'plans to prosper you and not to harm you, plans to give you hope and a future.'" – Jeremiah 29:11

"Blessed is the one who does not walk in step with the wicked or stand in the way that sinners take or sit in the company of mockers." – Psalm 1:1-2

"And Jesus grew in wisdom and stature, and in favor with God and man." – Luke 2:52

"Listen, my sons, to a father's instruction; pay attention and gain understanding." – Proverbs 4:1

Session 9

"And the God of all grace, who called you to His eternal glory in Christ, after you have suffered a little while, will Himself restore you and make you strong, firm, and steadfast." – I Peter 5:10

Session 10

"They celebrate Your abundant goodness and joyfully sing of Your righteousness." – Psalm 145:7

Cathy has over eleven years of experience in the recovery field as the ministry leader for Celebrate Recovery (CR) at her church, where she is also a pastor and counselor. She has served as the California State Representative for CR in Los Angeles and Orange Counties for the past seven years.

Her own experience as a Hurting Mom, along with her extensive work in recovery, give her a personal perspective that she shares openly and transparently in a way that offers hope, healing, and restoration to other women who are struggling.

Invite Cathy to speak to your group about a host of topics related to recovery, addiction, or being a Hurting Mom.

Go to www.hurtingmoms.com/contact to book Cathy for a speaking engagement.

www.SquareTreePublishing.com

www.HurtingMoms.com

SQUARE TREE PUBLISHING
RESOURCES

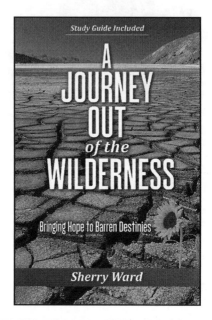

ENCOURAGEMENT YOU NEED TO MAKE IT THROUGH A WILDERNESS SEASON OF LIFE!

A Journey Out of the Wilderness is for people going through a rough time – a Wilderness experience – where you feel as though you are "down for the count" and ready to give up. You ask yourself, "Will this ever end?", however, being in the Wilderness will be one of the most transformational times of your life.

Sherry Lynn Ward's book is filled with insights and revelations God gave her in the Wilderness. Her heart is to help the hurting, those who need the courage to keep going despite the circumstances. Whether you have a wayward child, a broken marriage, or financial difficulties, *A Journey Out of the Wilderness* offers hope and encouragement. You will make it out of your Wilderness and be launched into your destiny and into your own personal Promised Land!

For encouraging blogs go to **www.SherryLynnWard.com**
View this and more at **www.SquareTreePublishing.com**

At **SQUARE TREE PUBLISHING,** we believe your message matters. That is why our dedicated team of professionals is committed to bringing your literary texts and targeted curriculum to a global marketplace. We strive to make that message of the highest quality, while still maintaining your voice. We believe in you, therefore, we provide a platform through website design, blogs, and social media campaigns to showcase your unique message. Our innovative team offers a full range of services: from editing to graphic design, inspired with an eye for excellence so your message is clearly and distinctly heard.

Whether you are a new writer needing guidance with each step of the process, or a seasoned writer, we will propel you to the next level of your development.

At **SQUARE TREE PUBLISHING,** it's all about **you.**

Take advantage of a free consultation.
Your opportunity is "Write Outside the Box"!

www.SquareTreePublishing.com

www.HurtingMoms.com

Made in the USA
San Bernardino, CA
18 February 2016